Learning to Walk with Jesus
Vineyard Columbus

Published 2017 by
Vineyard Columbus
6000 Cooper Rd
Westerville, Ohio 43081

vineyardcolumbus.org
bookstore@vineyardcolumbus.org

© Vineyard Columbus
All rights reserved. No part of this publication may be reproduced, stored in a retrieval system or transmitted, in any form or by any means, electronic, mechanical, photocopying, recording or otherwise, without the prior written permission of the copyright owner.

Scripture quotations marked (NIV) are taken from the Holy Bible, New International Version ®, NIV ®. Copyright © 1973, 1978, 1984, 2011 by Biblica, Inc. TM Used by permission of Zondervan. All rights reserved worldwide. www.zondervan.com The "NIV" and "New International Version" are trademarks registered in the United States Patent and Trademark Office by Biblica, Inc. TM

Table of Contents

4	I've Decided to Follow Jesus...Now What?
6	**Five-Day Devotional: The Big Story**
9	Act 1 - Once Upon A Time
19	Act 2 - The Fall
29	Act 3 - The Promise
37	Act 4 - The Rescue
38	Scene 1
40	Scene 2
42	Scene 3
44	Scene 4
49	Act 5 - Happily Ever After

56 Twenty-Day Devotional: Growing as a Christian
    Membership
60   Day 1
64   Day 2
68   Day 3
72   Day 4
    Maturity
80   Day 1
84   Day 2
88   Day 3
92   Day 4
    Meeting God
100   Day 1
104   Day 2
108   Day 3
112   Day 4
    Ministry
120   Day 1
124   Day 2
128   Day 3
1132   Day 4
    Mission
140   Day 1
144   Day 2
148   Day 3
152   Day 4

I've Decided to Follow Jesus...
Now What?

Congratulations on making the decision to follow Christ! You have made the most important decision of your life. You prayed and asked Jesus to come into your heart, but what does that mean exactly? Well, this is where this devotional, Learning to Walk with Jesus, can help you. This devotional is designed to help you better understand the Christian faith and to help you learn how to walk with God. It will show you what it looks like for you to be a follower of Jesus.

So what exactly is a devotional? Christians use devotionals as a way to grow closer to God and learn more about the Christian life. Devotional books are not meant to be read in one sitting. They are designed for you to read a bit every day, so you can slowly learn to apply what you read to your own life and learn how to pray on a consistent basis. By praying every day, you will develop a stronger relationship with God. In this devotional, you are going to find scriptures, encouraging words, and prayers that will guide you on how you can begin your new life. If you do not have a Bible, you can stop by the Information Counter in the lobby during any of our services and get one free. You can also download a free Bible app on your phone or tablet at Bible.com.

In Learning to Walk with Jesus, we use Vineyard Columbus' mission statement to help you understand what it looks like for you to grow. Our mission as a church is to develop a community of disciples who experience God, love one another, and partner with Christ to heal the world. Every few months Vineyard Columbus has what we call growth classes. In these five classes we learn how to live out our mission statement in our daily lives. The classes cover the importance of community, what it means to be a disciple of Jesus, how we can experience God, how we can use our gifts, and how we partner with Jesus to love the world. We use these topics to illustrate how you can begin living out this mission statement as well.

Your desire to follow Christ is the beginning of a journey. The reason we use the word 'walk' when we refer to our lives with Jesus is that this lifestyle is a "walk and not a sprint." It takes time to understand the Bible. It might take time to get comfortable at church or to change habits. At our church we use the term "left foot, right foot," meaning we walk in this life with Jesus step by step. It can be overwhelming and exciting all at the same time. Remember that Jesus is right here with you, each step of the way; not to make sure you don't do anything wrong, but to care for you. He is here to give you love, encouragement, grace, and forgiveness.

We are so excited for your new journey and for all that God has in store for you!

God Bless,

The Vineyard Columbus Outreach and Connect Ministry

The Big Story

Who is God? Why am I here? Does God care about me? Will good triumph over evil? What does the future hold? These are important questions that in one way or another each of us spend our lives trying to answer. Some of the best insight on these matters is found within the pages of the Bible. But how can you begin to understand something that contains 66 books spanning more than one thousand years? Where do you start? There are countless stories, poems, genealogies, instructions, rules, counsel, history, letters, prophecies, eyewitness testimonies, etc. It's overwhelming and at times confusing!

This five-day devotional, which follows the pattern of a five-act play, will tell you something of the beginning, the middle, and the end of the story found in the Bible. As the long and important saga unfolds, we will land on five pivotal moments in scripture so as to offer a succinct version of the most important story in the universe. It's a story of God's creative power, perfect holiness and astounding love – love for you, all of humanity, and everything he's ever created. And like any good play, there's drama. Something goes wrong, a hero emerges, and so do some answers to your big questions.

Act 1

Learning to Walk with Jesus

Once Upon a Time

The Big Story
Act 1 – Once Upon a Time
Genesis 1

1 In the beginning God created the heavens and the earth. **2** Now the earth was formless and empty, darkness was over the surface of the deep, and the Spirit of God was hovering over the waters.

3 And God said, "Let there be light," and there was light. **4** God saw that the light was good, and he separated the light from the darkness. **5** God called the light "day," and the darkness he called "night." And there was evening, and there was morning—the first day.

6 And God said, "Let there be a vault between the waters to separate water from water." **7** So God made the vault and separated the water under the vault from the water above it. And it was so. **8** God called the vault "sky." And there was evening, and there was morning—the second day.

9 And God said, "Let the water under the sky be gathered to one place, and let dry ground appear." And it was so. **10** God called the dry ground "land," and the gathered waters he called "seas." And God saw that it was good.

11 Then God said, "Let the land produce vegetation: seed-bearing plants and trees on the land that bear fruit with seed in it, according to their various kinds." And it was so. **12** The land produced vegetation: plants bearing seed according to their kinds and trees bearing fruit with seed in it according to their kinds. And God saw that it was good. **13** And there was evening, and there was morning—the third day.

14 And God said, "Let there be lights in the vault of the sky to separate the day from the night, and let them serve as signs to mark sacred times, and days and years, **15** and let them be lights in the vault of the sky to give light on the earth." And it was so. **16** God made two great lights—the greater light to govern the day and the lesser light to govern the night. He also made the stars. **17** God set them in the vault of the sky to give light on the earth, **18** to govern the day and the night, and to separate light from darkness. And God saw that it was good. **19** And there was evening, and there was morning—the fourth day.

20 And God said, "Let the water teem with living creatures, and let birds fly above the earth across the vault of the sky." **21** So God created the great creatures of the sea and every living thing with which the water teems and that moves about in it, according to their kinds, and every winged bird according to its kind. And God saw that it was good. **22** God blessed them and said, "Be fruitful and increase in number and fill the water in the seas, and let the birds increase on the earth." **23** And there was evening, and there was morning—the fifth day.

24 And God said, "Let the land produce living creatures according to their kinds: the livestock, the creatures that move along the ground, and the wild animals, each according to its kind." And it was so. **25** God made the wild animals according to their kinds, the livestock according to their kinds, and all the creatures that move along the ground according to their kinds. And God saw that it was good.

26 Then God said, "Let us make mankind in our image, in our likeness, so that they may rule over the fish in the sea and the birds in the sky, over the livestock and all the wild animals, and over all the creatures that move along the ground."

27 So God created mankind in his own image,
in the image of God he created them;
male and female he created them.

28 God blessed them and said to them, "Be fruitful and increase in number; fill the earth and subdue it. Rule over

Learning to Walk with Jesus

The Big Story
Act 1 – Once Upon a Time
Genesis 1

the fish in the sea and the birds in the sky and over every living creature that moves on the ground."

29 Then God said, "I give you every seed-bearing plant on the face of the whole earth and every tree that has fruit with seed in it. They will be yours for food. **30** And to all the beasts of the earth and all the birds in the sky and all the creatures that move along the ground—everything that has the breath of life in it—I give every green plant for food." And it was so.

31 God saw all that he had made, and it was very good. And there was evening, and there was morning—the sixth day.

The Big Story
Act 1 – Once Upon a Time

When God, who existed before anything else, created the universe, it was good. Even the account here in Genesis 1 is good. In a beautiful and poetic narrative, it describes an incredibly complex and lengthy process initiated and executed by God. While this didn't happen by chance, Genesis 1 is not a science textbook telling us exactly how it happened. Rather, it's like a love song testifying that God is good and all that he's created is good. He spoke and life sprung forth. It was good.

Why did God make the heavens, the earth, light, darkness, water, sky, land, plants, sun, moon, and animals? Because he abounds in creativity and enjoys beauty. We can see it all around us – a spectacular sunrise, vibrant spring flowers, breathtaking mountain ranges, melodic songbirds, a majestic deer bounding through freshly-fallen snow. It's all good.

Why did God create us? Because he wants to have a relationship with us. As a trinity – Father, Son, and Holy Spirit – God's very being is relational. Moreover, he had something unique in mind when he created us. We are God's image-bearers, the only aspect of his creation designated as such. This means there is something of God in each of us: his creativity, his goodness, etc. When God created us, he poured out parts of his very self, his very best. When each of us live in the fullness of our design, we experience his glory, the very best he has to offer. This includes harmony in all relationships: between God and us, creation and us, among one another, and with ourselves. It's good. Very good.

For reflection:

When God looks at you, what does he see? As his image-bearer, God's life is in you; at your core you are good. These are the things he sees. Perhaps you doubt whether that could be true, because when you look at yourself you feel like you don't measure up. You're not smart enough, not attractive enough, not successful enough, etc. These negative thoughts do not come from God. While he called creation "good," he didn't call it "very good" until he made people. This is both life-affirming and purpose-affirming. You are the crowning achievement of his creation.

God's creation and his creative nature, which dwells in each of us, are beautiful gifts. Here are a few suggestions for enjoying these gifts:

- Experience creation: Go for a walk, perhaps at a park or someplace else that takes you away from the sights and sounds of modernity. Pay close attention to all the flora and fauna you see. Think about how God created each of these things and just how enjoyable they are.

- Care for creation: Become more mindful of how to protect and improve creation. Pick up trash whenever you see it; support conservation initiatives; consume less; when you plan things – everything from parties to trips to landscaping -- research how to do it in ways that protect and improve creation.

- Be creative: Part of our identity as image-bearers of God is that we are designed to be creative, just as he is. Consider all the options we have for expressing our God-given creativity: the visual arts, literature, music, dance, theater, handicraft, cooking, decorating, designing etc. Even problem-solving of a very practical nature is an act of creativity!

The Big Story
Notes & Reflections

My concerns about the word "given to us" subdue the animals of the Earth.
What if it the other way around

The trees, Flora & Fauna Animals with their "unconditional love" are to be loved and cared for

I am just not sure, it too simplistic
I feel like there's more

Bible spanned 1000 yrs
much was before

Questions like the first
Bible —

Act 2

Learning to Walk with Jesus

The Fall

The Big Story
Act 2 – The Fall
Genesis 3

1 Now the serpent was more crafty than any of the wild animals the Lord God had made. He said to the woman, "Did God really say, 'You must not eat from any tree in the garden'?"

2 The woman said to the serpent, "We may eat fruit from the trees in the garden, **3** but God did say, 'You must not eat fruit from the tree that is in the middle of the garden, and you must not touch it, or you will die.'"

4 "You will not certainly die," the serpent said to the woman. **5** "For God knows that when you eat from it your eyes will be opened, and you will be like God, knowing good and evil."

6 When the woman saw that the fruit of the tree was good for food and pleasing to the eye, and also desirable for gaining wisdom, she took some and ate it. She also gave some to her husband, who was with her, and he ate it. **7** Then the eyes of both of them were opened, and they realized they were naked; so they sewed fig leaves together and made coverings for themselves.

8 Then the man and his wife heard the sound of the Lord God as he was walking in the garden in the cool of the day, and they hid from the Lord God among the trees of the garden. **9** But the Lord God called to the man, "Where are you?"

10 He answered, "I heard you in the garden, and I was afraid because I was naked; so I hid."

11 And he said, "Who told you that you were naked? Have you eaten from the tree that I commanded you not to eat from?"

12 The man said, "The woman you put here with me—she gave me some fruit from the tree, and I ate it."
13 Then the Lord God said to the woman, "What is this you have done?"

The woman said, "The serpent deceived me, and I ate."
14 So the Lord God said to the serpent, "Because you have done this,

"Cursed are you above all livestock
   and all wild animals!
You will crawl on your belly
   and you will eat dust
   all the days of your life.
15 And I will put enmity
   between you and the woman,
   and between your offspring and hers;
he will crush your head,
   and you will strike his heel."
16 To the woman he said,
"I will make your pains in childbearing very severe;
   with painful labor you will give birth to children.
Your desire will be for your husband,
   and he will rule over you."

The Big Story
Act 2 – The Fall
Genesis 3

17 To Adam he said, "Because you listened to your wife and ate fruit from the tree about which I commanded you, 'You must not eat from it,'

"Cursed is the ground because of you;
    through painful toil you will eat food from it
    all the days of your life.
18 It will produce thorns and thistles for you,
    and you will eat the plants of the field.
19 By the sweat of your brow
    you will eat your food
until you return to the ground,
    since from it you were taken;
for dust you are
    and to dust you will return."
20 Adam named his wife Eve, because she would become the mother of all the living.

21 The Lord God made garments of skin for Adam and his wife and clothed them. **22** And the Lord God said, "The man has now become like one of us, knowing good and evil. He must not be allowed to reach out his hand and take also from the tree of life and eat, and live forever." **23** So the Lord God banished him from the Garden of Eden to work the ground from which he had been taken. **24** After he drove the man out, he placed on the east side of the Garden of Eden cherubim and a flaming sword flashing back and forth to guard the way to the tree of life.

The Big Story
Act 2 – The Fall

Evil. Deceit. Rebellion. Fear. Blame-shifting. Consequences. Anyone who hasn't experienced or committed any of these things is living under a rock. We don't have to search very long or hard to see that there's something wrong with the world. Sometimes, we need only look at ourselves.

As we read in verse 1, the disruption of God's perfect creation seems to have begun with Satan, a spiritual being here embodied as a serpent. He is the accuser, a chief adversary of both God and humanity. God will always tell us the truth; he always seeks our good. Meanwhile, Satan always lies; he seeks our destruction. He wants to ruin every good thing God gave to humanity: our unhindered connection to the divine, harmonious relationships, our ability to thrive, the beauty of creation, etc.

One of the ways Satan particularly afflicts humanity is by causing us to doubt God's plan and good intentions for us. "Did God really say….?" Satan planted a seed of doubt in the human heart, beginning with Adam and Eve, which yielded the sins of rebellion, fear and blame-shifting, followed by consequences that are still felt to this day.

When Adam and Eve rebelled by eating from the one tree God told them not to, what they were communicating to God was, "We reject your good plan. We choose to shun your amazing love." As the story proceeds, things fall apart even more: they were suddenly afraid to be around God; Eve blamed Satan for their rebellion, Adam blamed Eve.

The consequences of Satan, Adam and Eve's actions are known as "the curse." Harm came to humanity in a multitude of ways: pain and sorrow in childbearing and childrearing, oppressive gender dynamics, toilsome back-breaking labor, banishment from both paradise and God's unencumbered presence. The curse also meant the ultimate expression of pain and sorrow – physical death – would be the inevitable fate of every living thing. And yet! God wove some hope into the curse. In verse 15, when he told the serpent "he will crush your head," this was a nod to a time when evil would be defeated by our great rescuer.

For reflection:

- Although it happened so long ago, do you feel the weight of the earliest manifestation of evil and the first sin in your own life? What about when you look out on the world? How do you think God feels about his creation gone awry?

- Do you fear being close to God or allowing him to see your true self? Do you doubt his good intentions for you and all of creation? Do you reject his plan? If you answered "yes" to any of the above, consider why. Imagine and write down what it would be like to move from a place of fear to a place of trust.

The Big Story
Notes & Reflections

Act 3

Learning to Walk with Jesus

The Promise

The Big Story
Act 3 – The Promise
Genesis 12:1-9

1 The Lord had said to Abram, "Go from your country, your people and your father's household to the land I will show you.

2 "I will make you into a great nation,
   and I will bless you;
I will make your name great,
   and you will be a blessing.
3 I will bless those who bless you,
   and whoever curses you I will curse;
and all peoples on earth
   will be blessed through you."

4 So Abram went, as the Lord had told him; and Lot went with him. Abram was seventy-five years old when he set out from Harran. **5** He took his wife Sarai, his nephew Lot, all the possessions they had accumulated and the people they had acquired in Harran, and they set out for the land of Canaan, and they arrived there.

6 Abram traveled through the land as far as the site of the great tree of Moreh at Shechem. At that time the Canaanites were in the land. **7** The Lord appeared to Abram and said, "To your offspring I will give this land." So he built an altar there to the Lord, who had appeared to him.
8 From there he went on toward the hills east of Bethel and pitched his tent, with Bethel on the west and Ai on the east. There he built an altar to the Lord and called on the name of the Lord.

9 Then Abram set out and continued toward the Negev.

The Big Story
Act 3 – The Promise

"All peoples on earth will be blessed through you." After the fall in Genesis 3, sin exponentially multiplied, leading God to declare "that every inclination of the thoughts of the human heart was only evil all the time" (Genesis 6:5). But just a few chapters later God tells us humanity is in store for worldwide blessing. And it's supposed to come through the offspring of a seventy-five-year-old guy who doesn't even have kids. Is God really going to rescue us from the mess we've gotten ourselves into? In this way? Yes! God is that good; he loves us that much; he is that faithful; he is that capable.

Being so relational in nature, God's primary way of telling the whole world about his promise wasn't a unilateral action such as writing it in the sky or erecting a giant statue. Rather, he planned to tell the whole world via a group of flawed people. He wanted to gather to himself a people who would testify about his goodness and his promise. These people became known as the Jewish nation of Israel.

When imperfect people are involved, things don't always go according to God's plan. Abraham and his equally aged wife Sarah took matters into their own hands to try starting a family. Sons deceived fathers. Brother abused brother. Men raped women. Prior to fulfillment of his promise, God needed to step in. He introduced The Ten Commandments and The Law to his people, tenets to follow for their good and the good of others; something to protect them from making more and more messes of their lives. Judges and kings helped the Israelites stay within these lanes of God's goodness. The Law also put a spotlight on humanity's deep need for the promise's eventual fulfillment.

Basically, God wanted the people to see that everything was centered around the promise. He gave them the opportunity to keep it at the forefront of their hearts by sending prophets over and over again to call them back to their purpose: blessed to be a blessing. Even miraculous events and significant moments in the lives of key Old Testament figures pointed to it. And yet, the fall meant one thing was certain: the nation of Israel would reject God and his promise, again and again. God would get very angry, but he would welcome his people back into his presence and keep directing their attention toward the promise. It was a seemingly never-ending cycle. One that would one day finally be broken by a rescuer. Cue Act Four.

For reflection:

- Have you ever had to wait a very long time for something eagerly anticipated? Kids undoubtedly feel this way about Christmas morning; pregnant women past their due date definitely do! Write down what your emotions, thoughts and actions are like while you're waiting. How patient are you? How do you think the Israelites and the rest of the world felt as they waited for God to save the day?

The Big Story
Notes & Reflections

Act 4

Learning to Walk with Jesus

The Rescue

The Big Story
Act 4 – The Rescue

In the following scenes, we see how Jesus Christ, the son of God, arrives to bring about the climax of the story of the Bible.

Scene One – John 1:1-5

1 In the beginning was the Word, and the Word was with God, and the Word was God. **2** He was with God in the beginning. **3** Through him all things were made; without him nothing was made that has been made. **4** In him was life, and that life was the light of all mankind. **5** The light shines in the darkness, and the darkness has not overcome it.

Whenever you see "word" capitalized in scripture, it's not in reference to something written; it's not about the Bible. The Word is a person. He's someone divine who's been around since the beginning, hanging out with Father God and the Holy Spirit.

When God made his promise to Abraham, it wasn't an "I'll figure out how to keep my word as I go along" type of promise. God knew exactly how he was going to fulfill his promise, bless all nations, heal the entire world from the devastation of the fall and crush Satan's head (Genesis 3:15). He would do it all through The Word.

The Word is our rescuer. He's the embodiment of the promise fulfilled, the perfect representation of everything God has ever said. He is life; he is light. And no matter how dark things seem – through consequences of your own actions, forces beyond your control, harm done to you, etc. – darkness cannot overcome the light. When it's all said and done, that is one thing we can be certain will never happen. And at this point in the story, the light is going to shine brighter than ever before

For reflection:

- Jot down a list of the benefits of light, both for people and nature. What do you think "light" means in a spiritual context? How might it be helpful? What about "darkness"; what does it mean in a spiritual context?

Notes & Reflections

The Big Story
Act 4 – The Rescue
Scene Two – John 17:1-5

1 After Jesus said this, he looked toward heaven and prayed:

"Father, the hour has come. Glorify your Son, that your Son may glorify you. **2** For you granted him authority over all people that he might give eternal life to all those you have given him. **3** Now this is eternal life: that they know you, the only true God, and Jesus Christ, whom you have sent. **4** I have brought you glory on earth by finishing the work you gave me to do. **5** And now, Father, glorify me in your presence with the glory I had with you before the world began.

The Word, whom John introduced at the very beginning of his gospel narrative, is Jesus Christ of Nazareth: a descendent of Abraham, God's Son, the savior of the world, the rescuer. Here he is, knowing he's in the final moments of his life, praying to his Father in heaven. His mission is almost complete.

Jesus is asking for God to pour out his best upon him. Even as he walks toward death, Jesus knows he can experience God's presence and reassurance. He also reveals the way to eternal life, how we can be rescued from the destruction of the fall: know God, know Jesus. Jesus came to earth and found us in our messes and our pain and said, "I love you! I will rescue you! Come; get to know me and get to know God."

For reflection:

- What do you think it would take to know God and Jesus in the way someone knows a beloved spouse or friend? What do you think it means to know Jesus as your rescuer, as the promise-fulfiller? If you feel led, open yourself to this journey of knowing.

Notes & Reflections

The Big Story
Act 4 – The Rescue
Scene Three – John 19:28–30

28 Later, knowing that everything had now been finished, and so that Scripture would be fulfilled, Jesus said, "I am thirsty." **29** A jar of wine vinegar was there, so they soaked a sponge in it, put the sponge on a stalk of the hyssop plant, and lifted it to Jesus' lips. **30** When he had received the drink, Jesus said, "It is finished." With that, he bowed his head and gave up his spirit.

Jesus is nailed to a cross, moments from death. How did he get here, to this horrific demise? The simple explanation is this: Roman government officials and Jewish religious experts alike wanted him dead. He was too powerful; he was causing too much of a stir. But how can this be? The person who's supposed to rescue us can't die! This is not light; this is deepest darkness!

Notice the line, "so that scripture would be fulfilled." The fuller answer to "how can this be?" is that it was part of God's plan all along. Hundreds of years prior to the crucifixion, he spoke through prophets about this day. Even scenes in the Old Testament such as Passover (Exodus 12), when the Israelites were trying to escape enslavement in Egypt, point to this moment. The plagues "passed over" Israelite households because they put the blood of a sacrificial lamb on their door frames.

Because of Jesus' sacrifice, death can pass over us. In his death, Jesus took on all evil, all punishment for sin, so we can go free. He is the sacrificial lamb. We're no longer left to our own devices, trying to be a "good person" – we can stop hopelessly trying to prove ourselves to God. We no longer have to work for his love. And because we don't earn God's love, we can never lose it. There are no more hoops, like rituals and sacrifices of the Old Testament, to jump through in order to enjoy God's presence. Jesus' sacrifice means we can freely receive the love, grace, and mercy of God. Jesus is the promise-fulfiller! He's the rescuer! The fallout of sin is no more.

For reflection:

- Jesus, especially in the gospel of John, talks a lot about his role as a suffering servant, as the one willing to lose it all because of how much he loves us. In his suffering, he took on the sins of the world and he took on your sins. What he did was extraordinarily personal. As you consider this, how does it make you feel? Write down your response.

Notes & Reflections

The Big Story
Act 4 – The Rescue
Scene Four: John 20:11-18

11 Now Mary stood outside the tomb crying. As she wept, she bent over to look into the tomb **12** and saw two angels in white, seated where Jesus' body had been, one at the head and the other at the foot.

13 They asked her, "Woman, why are you crying?"
"They have taken my Lord away," she said, "and I don't know where they have put him." **14** At this, she turned around and saw Jesus standing there, but she did not realize that it was Jesus.

15 He asked her, "Woman, why are you crying? Who is it you are looking for?"

Thinking he was the gardener, she said, "Sir, if you have carried him away, tell me where you have put him, and I will get him."

16 Jesus said to her, "Mary."
She turned toward him and cried out in Aramaic, "Rabboni!" (which means "Teacher").

17 Jesus said, "Do not hold on to me, for I have not yet ascended to the Father. Go instead to my brothers and tell them, 'I am ascending to my Father and your Father, to my God and your God.'"

18 Mary Magdalene went to the disciples with the news: "I have seen the Lord!" And she told them that he had said these things to her.

The epic battle toward the end of a blockbuster action or fantasy movie typically gets lots of screen time. Similarly, we've devoted a lot of space to Act 4 of The Big Story. And this is the very best part: the climax!

At the beginning of this scene, Jesus' friends are really, really bummed. Yes, they are grieving their loved one, but they are also incredibly confused. They thought he was the Messiah, God's anointed one, the one who would save them. Messiahs don't die; they conquer.

When Mary, one of Jesus' close friends, visits his tomb, she is in for the surprise of her life. Jesus' body is gone, and in its place are two angels. In her shock, she mistakes Jesus for the tomb gardener. Not until Jesus says her name does she realize the truth: he's alive! This speaks to the incredibly personal nature of Jesus and what it means to be in a relationship with him. Mary is known by Jesus – deeply known. It's a really special, personal thing to be truly known by someone. Many of us start our journey toward Jesus by hearing his voice and beginning to respond to him. This relationship takes a turn toward incredible intimacy and knowing when you hear him say your name.

Also, it's one thing for God to tell us that in Jesus' death we can have eternal life, but quite another for Jesus to show us that he has indeed defeated death. About Christ's resurrection, the Apostle Paul, a later follower of Jesus, says in 1 Corinthians, "Where, O death is your victory? Where, O death is your sting?" Jesus has the certain victory!

For reflection:

- Take another look at verse 16, when Jesus calls Mary by her name. How do you think you would respond to Jesus calling you by your name? Imagine him saying to you, "Come away with me. Come back to paradise, where death is no more. Forever share in my victory. Enjoy my presence. Enjoy being deeply known. Enjoy the presence of all God's people." What will you say to him?

The Big Story
Notes & Reflections

Act 5

Learning to Walk with Jesus

Happily Ever After

The Big Story
Act 5 – Happily Ever After
Revelation 21:1-8

1 Then I saw "a new heaven and a new earth," for the first heaven and the first earth had passed away, and there was no longer any sea. **2** I saw the Holy City, the new Jerusalem, coming down out of heaven from God, prepared as a bride beautifully dressed for her husband. **3** And I heard a loud voice from the throne saying, "Look! God's dwelling place is now among the people, and he will dwell with them. They will be his people, and God himself will be with them and be their God. **4** 'He will wipe every tear from their eyes. There will be no more death' or mourning or crying or pain, for the old order of things has passed away."

5 He who was seated on the throne said, "I am making everything new!" Then he said, "Write this down, for these words are trustworthy and true."

6 He said to me: "It is done. I am the Alpha and the Omega, the Beginning and the End. To the thirsty I will give water without cost from the spring of the water of life. **7** Those who are victorious will inherit all this, and I will be their God and they will be my children. **8** But the cowardly, the unbelieving, the vile, the murderers, the sexually immoral, those who practice magic arts, the idolaters and all liars—they will be consigned to the fiery lake of burning sulfur. This is the second death."

The Big Story
Act 5 – Happily Ever After

If death was defeated by Jesus in the climax of Act 4, why do people still die? Why does tragedy still strike? Why aren't things perfect like they were for Adam and Eve in the garden? Because Jesus hasn't finished what he started – we await the full resolution of the story. When he returns, he will defeat all evil. That's what the "then" at the beginning of this passage refers to. One chapter prior, in Revelation 20, we read that Jesus defeats the devil – Satan, the accuser, the adversary, the same being that sought to destroy Adam and Eve in the beginning. The new heaven and earth described here will come to pass after the final battle of good vs evil.

While Jesus, in his death and resurrection, offers us spiritual life and renewal, we still grapple with the effects of the fall in many ways. Sadness, evil, death, and pain come upon everyone from individuals to humanity as a whole. Even something like the demise of a houseplant or death of a pet can tell us that things are not as they should be.

Jesus inaugurated a new era when he died and rose again, but it has not yet been brought to completion. That will happen upon his second return. In the Apostle John's dramatic and symbolic vision described in the final pages of the Bible, we get a glimpse of what things will be like when Jesus comes back. Contrary to popular lore, people will not float around on clouds playing harps. We will be together on earth, in a beautiful city complete with an idyllic garden, which harkens back to Genesis 1, God's original plan for humanity. God will come to dwell with us. We will interact with him face-to-face. We'll never be sad again; no one and nothing will die; pain will cease. Peace will prevail.

Verse five tells us that Jesus is in the business of transformation. He started the job when he rose from the dead; you may sense this shift in your own life. And just as God fulfilled his promise to Abraham, so will he fulfill his promise to finish the work and "make everything new." The defeat of death and the renewal of all things begin and end with Jesus.

Not only will death be no more, but verse eight indicates there will also be no evil in this eternal city. If evils such as trauma or abuse have ever been afflicted on you or a loved one, rest assured that unrepentant perpetrators and forces of evil have no place in the new heaven and new earth. This is such good news for survivors and those suffering from PTSD. Forevermore, you will be safe.

For reflection:

- Imagine yourself in this new city, fully experiencing the completion of Jesus' mission. What do you see? What do you hear? How do you feel? How do you think God feels to see you there? Imagine no longer having to carry around burdens of deep sorrow, regret, alienation, and grief. Imagine no longer fearing for your health, well-being, and safety. Imagine never again being afraid or anxious. It is almost beyond comprehension. Return to this visualization from time to time; as you do so, may you grow in passion and hunger for the completion of Jesus' work.

- Philosopher Alasdair MacIntyre said, "I can only answer the question, 'What am I to do?' if I can answer the prior question, 'Of what story do I find myself a part?'" What big life questions have been answered as you've read through The Big Story? Do you have any new questions? Perhaps they will be answered in the 20-day devotional that follows this one. Either way, keep asking questions, and keep seeking God for answers.

The Big Story
Notes & Reflections

20-Day Devotional
Growing as a Christian

Everyone has a next step to take in their faith journey. Take yours by reading through this 20-day devotional that introduces you to different ways you can grow spiritually. Divided into five topics – Membership, Maturity, Meeting God, Ministry, and Mission – this will also familiarize you with themes of the Vineyard Growth classes.

Membership

Learning to Walk with Jesus

We are a Community

Why church?

In this first section, you'll get familiar with the importance of Christian community and learn about Vineyard Columbus' values as a church.

Growing as a Christian
1.1 New Life, New Love
1 John 3:1-17

1 Now there was a Pharisee, a man named Nicodemus who was a member of the Jewish ruling council. **2** He came to Jesus at night and said, "Rabbi, we know that you are a teacher who has come from God. For no one could perform the signs you are doing if God were not with him."
3 Jesus replied, "Very truly I tell you, no one can see the kingdom of God unless they are born again."
4 "How can someone be born when they are old?" Nicodemus asked. "Surely they cannot enter a second time into their mother's womb to be born!"
5 Jesus answered, "Very truly I tell you, no one can enter the kingdom of God unless they are born of water and the Spirit. **6** Flesh gives birth to flesh, but the Spirit gives birth to spirit. **7** You should not be surprised at my saying, 'You must be born again.' **8** The wind blows wherever it pleases. You hear its sound, but you cannot tell where it comes from or where it is going. So it is with everyone born of the Spirit."
9 "How can this be?" Nicodemus asked.
10 "You are Israel's teacher," said Jesus, "and do you not understand these things? **11** Very truly I tell you, we speak of what we know, and we testify to what we have seen, but still you people do not accept our testimony. **12** I have spoken to you of earthly things and you do not believe; how then will you believe if I speak of heavenly things? **13** No one has ever gone into heaven except the one who came from heaven—the Son of Man. **14** Just as Moses lifted up the snake in the wilderness, so the Son of Man must be lifted up, **15** that everyone who believes may have eternal life in him."
16 For God so loved the world that he gave his one and only Son, that whoever believes in him shall not perish but have eternal life. **17** For God did not send his Son into the world to condemn the world, but to save the world through him.

Something is new. You see things – who Jesus is and what role he plays in your life – differently. Maybe it was a really dramatic encounter. Perhaps it was a steady and slow progression toward Jesus. Or maybe this feels like an accident, something you've stumbled upon. No matter the route, here you are, with this book in your hands, beginning to seek God via the Bible either for the first time; or once again after a long hiatus.

Look at this Bible passage, John 3:1-17, with fresh eyes. Maybe you've heard a televangelist preach about being "born again." Perhaps you've seen "John 3:16" on a highway overpass among lots of other graffiti. Let those impressions slip out of your mind and instead imagine hearing these words of Jesus and John for the first time.

Jesus is offering us something entirely new. To be "born again" is to experience a critical shift within your spirit, initiated by God. He's opened your eyes to his offer of new life, and you've grabbed hold of it. It's flooded your soul. The greatest "do-over" the world has ever known has been given to you. And it's still there, abounding in power to bring continual renewal to your life!

Not only do we experience new life, but also new love. Verses 16-17 tell us Jesus loves us – you, your friends, the entire world – so very much, that he is willing to die for us. This is love like no other. We don't deserve it, but he's not going to let that get in the way of offering it to us.

This isn't about rule-following. No assembly required; no prerequisites; no disqualifications. You don't have to do anything, just believe the good news found in John 3.

Growing as a Christian

For reflection:

- If you haven't yet made a commitment to Christ and sense a stirring in your heart to do so, speak this prayer to God: "Dear God, without you, I can't live life to the fullest. I've missed the mark; I've shunned your amazing love; I've sinned. Please forgive me. I believe Jesus Christ is your divine son. When he died on the cross for me, he defeated the power of sin. And then, he rose to life! By your grace, I join him in eternal life, where I can forever dwell in your loving presence. Thank you, God! From this day forward, through life's ups and downs, help me to trust Jesus as my saviour and Lord of every area of my life. Fill me with your Holy Spirit and lead me into your love, power, and holiness. In Jesus' name I pray, amen."

- Write down words and phrases from this Bible passage or the above prayer that really speak to your heart. As you continue on with this devotional, return to them from time to time, asking God to seal their truths in your spirit.

Alpha: A Next Step

Want to learn more about core beliefs of Christianity in a group setting? Try Alpha, a ten-week series exploring the Christian faith. Each talk looks at a different question around faith and is designed to create conversation. It is a laid back, pressure-free environment where you can discuss how you personally feel about topics relating to Christianity. Email alpha@vineyardcolumbus.org for more information.

Notes & Reflections

Growing as a Christian

1.2 Passionate Worship
John 12:1-3

1 Six days before the Passover, Jesus came to Bethany, where Lazarus lived, whom Jesus had raised from the dead. **2** Here a dinner was given in Jesus' honor. Martha served, while Lazarus was among those reclining at the table with him. **3** Then Mary took about a pint of pure nard, an expensive perfume; she poured it on Jesus' feet and wiped his feet with her hair. And the house was filled with the fragrance of the perfume.

Christians place a high value on worshipping God. When we sing spiritual songs, we seek to change the atmosphere – to orient our hearts away from the things of this world, such as a hectic day or long to-do list, and toward God. Our gatherings often begin with singing songs to God. Songs have been sung about God for ages. Thousands of years ago in the Old Testament, when God parted the Red Sea so the nation of Israel could escape their enslavers, people sang about it. When an angel visited Mary to tell her she was pregnant with Jesus the Messiah, she sang about the goodness of God. Pick up any hymnal in the pew of an old church and you'll find plenty of songs about God: Amazing Grace, It is Well with My Soul, Blessed Assurance, etc. Singing these songs is a great way to express love for God, but there is a more intimate approach: sing to him.

Singing to God reflects the nearness we have to the divine; something Jesus has given to us. It's a wonderful way to enter into his presence. In this brief story found in the gospel of John, Jesus' friend Mary worships him passionately and intimately. Expensive perfume poured out on Jesus' feet: this is passion! Wiping his feet with her hair: this is intimacy! Especially in an ancient culture where women covered their hair and avoided interacting with men who weren't family. Her act filled the house with the perfume's fragrance: this is what the atmosphere-changing nature of worship is like! Passion and desire for intimacy ought to reside in the hearts of those seeking more of Jesus. One of the reasons it's so beneficial and important to attend church every week is because it creates space to worship God.

Filling the space with the fragrance of intimate and

Growing as a Christian

passionate worship can happen anywhere. Singing together at church is a fragrant offering to God. Singing along to worship music while cooking dinner or driving in your car fills the space with praise. It doesn't matter if you can't hit the notes perfectly. We sing songs when we fall in love or experience other strong emotions; we don't let a lack of talent stop us. The way we express our feelings to God should be no different.

For reflection:

- The next time you attend church, take a few measures to worship God with greater intentionality and passion. First, prioritize this time of worship. Organize your schedule so that you arrive early enough to really engage with God via song. Settle in and quiet your heart before worship begins. Second, imagine Jesus is in the room and you are singing directly to him. Finally, incorporate your entire being into the experience. If you feel an urge to do something like raise your hands, clap, kneel, cry, dance, utter spontaneous words of praise, etc., let it happen. If you'd like to get a head start on this "assignment," give it a try by listening to some worship music at home. You can go to vineyardcolumbus.org/welcome playlist and hear some of the worship music we listen to at Vineyard Columbus..

Membership 101

If you want to know more about who we are and what we value, join us for the Membership 101 class. Learn about our history, beliefs, and ministries. This class is required for membership. For more information, visit vineyardcolumbus.org/next-steps.

Notes & Reflections

Growing as a Christian

1.3 Life Together
Acts 2:42-47

42 They devoted themselves to the apostles' teaching and to fellowship, to the breaking of bread and to prayer. **43** Everyone was filled with awe at the many wonders and signs performed by the apostles. **44** All the believers were together and had everything in common. **45** They sold property and possessions to give to anyone who had need. **46** Every day they continued to meet together in the temple courts. They broke bread in their homes and ate together with glad and sincere hearts, **47** praising God and enjoying the favor of all the people. And the Lord added to their number daily those who were being saved.

Going to a new church can be overwhelming, especially when you attend a large one such as Vineyard Columbus. It can also feel easy to get lost in the crowd. Attending church shouldn't reinforce the way society as a whole often leaves us feeling: lonely, isolated, unknown, uninspired, and unfulfilled. God, who made us in his image, hasn't designed us to live this way. He embodies relationship as the trinity – Father, Son, and Holy Spirit – and he wants us to live similarly, in authentic community. You don't have to remain an anonymous face in a sea of people; there's an opportunity to experience being truly known and knit into a community. How? Where? In a small group! Attending one is at the heart of our mission; we believe authentic community reflects the heart of God.

In this story, the author Luke tells us about some of the very first small groups of Jesus' followers. He outlines four of their characteristics: devotion to teaching, common life (fellowship), sharing a meal (breaking bread), and prayer. As you can see, small groups are not just Bible studies. Common life is a matter of hanging out and helping out – celebrating birthdays, getting together for playdates, dropping off a homemade dinner to new parents, rejoicing together, mourning together, etc. Sharing a meal, even something as simple as coffee and a snack, is an echo of when Jesus broke bread with his disciples. Then there's prayer; at each small group gathering we make time to wait on God to speak and guide us as we pray for one another. A small group is a regularly-scheduled time to intentionally engage all of these spiritual practices. It makes for a great rhythm as you learn to walk with Jesus. Often, if you're not in a group, it is a challenge to incorporate the practices into your spiritual journey.

It's not like being a family; we are a family: the family of God. Notice verses 44-46. Attending a weekend service is the big family reunion. A small group, on the other hand, is your immediate family – the place where we take care of one another. When you have a surplus of something – time, resources, talent, etc. – you can use it to help a group member in need. It's hard to give and receive like this when you're an unknown face in a huge crowd; small groups are what make this possible. It can seem a little weird to go to a stranger's house and sit around in a circle singing worship songs (remember a point from yesterday's devotional: almost all of our gatherings begin with worship!), studying the Bible and praying together. But aren't all families a little weird? Step outside your comfort zone and give a small group a try.

Learning to Walk with Jesus

Growing as a Christian

For reflection:

- If you're not yet in a small group, visit one this week. Check out the Small Group finder at vineyardcolumbus.org/small-groups. Search by location, campus affiliation, day, age range and group type. For more information on a particular group, there's a link to email the leader. Be patient as you seek a group that "clicks." It can take a few tries, and that's ok!

- If you're already in a group, reflect on the features outlined in this passage: teaching, common life, sharing a meal and prayer. How can you contribute? Volunteer to lead discussion, organize a special outing, bring a snack or commit to pray out loud for fellow members during prayer ministry time.

GroupLink

Ready to step out of your row at church and into a circle? Then GroupLink is for you! GroupLink is a two-hour event where people meet and connect with others in their area of town and stage of life to start a new small group or join an existing group. Staff and volunteers will be there to help you, and there is free childcare! Email smallgroups@vineyardcolumbus.org for more information.

Notes & Reflections

Growing as a Christian
1.4 Meaningful Rituals
Matthew 3:13-17

13 Then Jesus came from Galilee to the Jordan to be baptized by John. **14** But John tried to deter him, saying, "I need to be baptized by you, and do you come to me?"
15 Jesus replied, "Let it be so now; it is proper for us to do this to fulfill all righteousness." Then John consented.
16 As soon as Jesus was baptized, he went up out of the water. At that moment heaven was opened, and he saw the Spirit of God descending like a dove and alighting on him.
17 And a voice from heaven said, "This is my Son, whom I love; with him I am well pleased."

Church culture has really changed over the years; most churches tend to keep things casual. The pastor doesn't wear a fancy robe; you won't see a lot of "Sunday best" in the congregation. There aren't many rituals performed or symbols displayed. We dabble in liturgy, but it's not the foundation of most church services. An informal style is not objectively better, it's just how we feel led to engage God as a community. That said, there are two formal rites that are really important: baptism and communion.

Baptism is not only a public proclamation of your decision to follow Christ, but it's also symbolic of the life and freedom that God offers to us. In Genesis 1, God parted waters of life to bring creation into being. In Exodus, God's people escaped slavery when he parted the Red Sea. By going through the water, they came to freedom. Symbols and rituals matter. They help us regularly remember important things about God and we can often sense his presence while engaging in them.

Remembrance and acknowledgement plus the potential for a powerful encounter is an expression of the "Both-And" nature of God, which is something we highly value at Vineyard. Our senior pastor even wrote a book about it! Similar to what happened to Jesus, God's Spirit may come and powerfully minister to the person emerging from the waters of baptism. Sometimes, when you take communion alongside your brothers and sisters in Christ, you are moved to tears as you sense a deep communal connection to Jesus' suffering and death. Embrace these "Both-And" moments when they come; they will nourish your soul.

Growing as a Christian

Here in Matthew, notice how John resists baptizing Jesus, proclaiming, "Um, Jesus, are you serious? You're the Messiah, the savior of the world. And you want me to do this for you?!" But Jesus insists it be done, because he knows this is something his Father wants him to do; it's a matter of obedience. Followers of Christ seek to imitate him in all ways. That means we too should be baptized. The same goes for communion, a continual reminder that we are united in the power of his death. In Luke 22, Jesus tells us to do it in remembrance of him.

For reflection:

- When you participate in church rituals, it's more than just going through the motions. We take communion every week at church and baptism celebrations occur six times per year, thus giving you lots of opportunities to practice full engaging. Be present; be open to a powerful encounter with God; pay close attention to the words you recite, treating them as a corporate prayer to God; pray for each person who emerges from the waters of baptism.

Baptism Class

If you are a follower of Christ and you haven't been baptized, now's the time! In order to participate, attend one of the required baptism classes. See the insert for upcoming dates. For more information, email baptism@vineyardcolumbus.org.

Notes & Reflections

Growing as a Christian
Membership Memory Verses

What is a Memory Verse?

These are short Bible passages you can memorize and bring to mind when needed. They will prove helpful in your faith journey. At the conclusion of each week of this 20-day devotional, we'll provide some memory verses to summarize what we've covered. Read them multiple times and give memorization a try; singing the words to a familiar tune is a great way to get the words to stick in your mind.

John 10:10
The thief comes only to steal and kill and destroy; I have come that they may have life, and have it to the full.

Psalm 86:12
I will praise you, Lord my God, with all my heart;
    I will glorify your name forever.

Romans 12:4-5
4 For just as each of us has one body with many members, and these members do not all have the same function, **5** so in Christ we, though many, form one body, and each member belongs to all the others.

Romans 6:3-4
3 Or don't you know that all of us who were baptized into Christ Jesus were baptized into his death? **4** We were therefore buried with him through baptism into death in order that, just as Christ was raised from the dead through the glory of the Father, we too may live a new life.

Prayer

Lord, I understand that community is important for me to grow stronger in my walk with you. Please help me to draw closer to you in new ways and to develop true friendship and community. Amen

Maturity

Learning to Walk with Jesus

We are Disciples

What does it mean to be a disciple?

The journey toward maturity is one of engaging in spiritual practices that will help you to look more like Jesus. These devotionals cover some of the primary ways to pursue and display maturity and live as disciples of Christ.

Growing as a Christian
2.1 The Journey
Philippians 2:12-18

12 Therefore, my dear friends, as you have always obeyed—not only in my presence, but now much more in my absence—continue to work out your salvation with fear and trembling, **13** for it is God who works in you to will and to act in order to fulfill his good purpose.

14 Do everything without grumbling or arguing, **15** so that you may become blameless and pure, "children of God without fault in a warped and crooked generation." Then you will shine among them like stars in the sky **16** as you hold firmly to the word of life. And then I will be able to boast on the day of Christ that I did not run or labor in vain. **17** But even if I am being poured out like a drink offering on the sacrifice and service coming from your faith, I am glad and rejoice with all of you. **18** So you too should be glad and rejoice with me.

While not as physically obvious as something in nature, such as a butterfly's life cycle, the Christian life is one of metamorphosis. It's not static. Your faith doesn't begin and end with saying yes to Jesus. Rather, it's the launching point for a journey toward maturity in Christ. Have you ever heard that phrase, "the journey is the destination"? That's what it's like to pursue a life of Christian character. It's the most worthwhile journey you will ever take!

In today's passage, an excerpt from a letter the Apostle Paul wrote to one of the earliest churches, he's encouraging these believers to pursue maturity in Christ. Let's unpack the idea of "working out your salvation" (v 12). Jesus did the work of salvation (justification) for us when he died on the cross. He's the one who made it possible for humanity to reconnect with God for all eternity. For those who've accepted Christ, nothing can ever take justification away. But it doesn't end there. Another important component of Christianity is called sanctification (holiness). God wants us to partner with him as we journey toward becoming holy. He wants to build our character into a life that reflects Jesus. This is the process of "working out your salvation." God justifies us and sanctifies us. Justification happens the moment we say yes to Jesus; sanctification is a process. This is why, like you read in the introductory letter to this booklet, we often use the phrase "Left Foot, Right Foot" to describe the life of a Christian.

Imagine not losing your temper so easily. Imaging holding your tongue instead of saying something hurtful. Imagine not overspending all the time. Imagine always keeping your word. Imagine being able to forgive someone who has deeply hurt you. Imagine a thought life that is more

Learning to Walk with Jesus

Growing as a Christian

peaceful and pure. Imagine serving others instead of yourself. Imagine making dating and relationship choices that honor God and improve your well-being. When things don't go as planned, imagine responding calmly instead of in frustration. Wouldn't such a transformed life be amazing!?

The Christian life is one where habitual sin becomes less and less of a factor. This is God "working in you" (v 13) as you "hold firmly" (v 16) to Jesus. Yes, he saves us, but he's also the one who makes us holy, if we allow him to. God's "good purpose" (v 13) is mutually beneficial; as we mature, it pleases God and we will "shine like stars" (v 15). While growing in Christian character may be challenging at times, it is ultimately to our benefit. Life is unpredictable, but on the whole, the more spiritually mature we are, the better it goes.

For Reflection:

- We will address the how-tos of maturity over the next few days. For now, ask yourself: is this something I desire? In verse 12, Paul identifies a primary mark of maturity: willingness to do the right thing when no one's watching. Are you up for the challenge of allowing God to work in you so that you can experience this transformation? Ask God to search your thoughts, faults, motives, etc. Pray he'd give you a sincere desire to pursue maturity.

Maturity 201

If you sometimes feel stuck, feel spiritually dry, or feel like the Lord isn't speaking into your life anymore, join us at this class. Learn how to read the Bible more purposefully, pray more powerfully, and become a mature disciple of Christ. See the insert for upcoming dates. For more information, visit https://www.vineyardcolumbus.org/next-steps.

Notes & Reflections

Growing as a Christian
2.2 Prayer
Luke 18:9-14

9 To some who were confident of their own righteousness and looked down on everyone else, Jesus told this parable: **10** "Two men went up to the temple to pray, one a Pharisee and the other a tax collector. **11** The Pharisee stood by himself and prayed: 'God, I thank you that I am not like other people—robbers, evildoers, adulterers—or even like this tax collector. **12** I fast twice a week and give a tenth of all I get.'

13 "But the tax collector stood at a distance. He would not even look up to heaven, but beat his breast and said, 'God, have mercy on me, a sinner.'

14 "I tell you that this man, rather than the other, went home justified before God. For all those who exalt themselves will be humbled, and those who humble themselves will be exalted."

Everyone prays; even atheists. Those who aren't spiritual may deny it, but almost anyone facing an extreme situation will cry out in their heart, or even audibly, something like, "Please, God, please!" "No, God, no!" "Why, God, why?" When people don't know what else to do, when they're desperate, they pray.

Another time most people will pray – or at least pretend to do so – is at gatherings like weddings, funerals, holiday meals, etc. We close our eyes and bow our heads as the pastor prays a prayer that may sound somewhat familiar. We hold hands around the table and say a simple prayer at Thanksgiving.

Praying in these ways barely scratches the surface of the practice. Yes, it's fitting to cry out to God when desperate. John Wimber, the founder of the Vineyard movement, had a favorite crisis prayer: "O God, O God, O God, O God." And yes, reciting a scripted prayer is often what the situation calls for. But there's so much more to experience!

For the Christian pursuing maturity, prayer is often like a conversation between two friends. We don't approach God self-righteously and stiffly, as the Pharisee – a religious expert – here in Jesus' story does. We do it more like the tax collector – someone who was less interested in putting on a show and more interested in keeping it real. His prayer is both humble and passionate. It's good to follow his example: tell God what's on your mind; ask for advice and direction; ask for help. Remember, it's a conversation. We talk to God, and he talks to us. We sit in silence, giving God ample room to speak. Speaking with him like this helps us to mature in our faith.

Learning to Walk with Jesus

Growing as a Christian

Open your mind and heart to the possibility of a life rich in conversational, humble, and passionate prayer. It may be a bit out of your comfort zone; that's ok. Since practice is essential for maturity, you'll likely get more comfortable over time.

For reflection:

Begin setting aside five minutes per day to pray. Start today. Even if you haven't given God much thought all day or don't particularly feel like praying, he rejoices when we come to him. For this five-minute prayer, devote one minute to each of the following:
- Sit in silence. Listen before you speak.
- Express gratitude. Thank God for who he is and all that he's done and is doing.
- Repent. Own up to your sin and the harm it's caused. Receive God's forgiveness with confidence.
- Ask for whatever you wish. Don't hold back; be as passionate as the tax collector about your needs, loved one's needs, the world's needs, etc.
- Conclude with another minute of silence. Listen for God's reply to your prayer.

Write down some key points from your prayer, and come back to it later to see how God has responded to it. As you get used to a daily time of prayer, you may want to pray for longer than five minutes, change up the format, etc. As your overall faith matures, so will your prayer life. Enjoy the journey!

Notes & Reflections

Growing as a Christian
2.3 Reading the Bible
Psalm 119:97-104

97 Oh, how I love your law!
  I meditate on it all day long.
98 Your commands are always with me
  and make me wiser than my enemies.
99 I have more insight than all my teachers,
  for I meditate on your statutes.
100 I have more understanding than the elders,
  for I obey your precepts.
101 I have kept my feet from every evil path
  so that I might obey your word.
102 I have not departed from your laws,
  for you yourself have taught me.
103 How sweet are your words to my taste,
  sweeter than honey to my mouth!
104 I gain understanding from your precepts;
  therefore I hate every wrong path.

It's good to read the Bible. It's beneficial to your soul, your body, your mind, your relationships, your daily life, your everything! God's written word will tell you again and again just how much he loves you, how to get through hard times, how to be a blessing to others, etc. These are the words that we need to hear on a regular basis; it's the sort of message you won't get anywhere else. The more you read it, the more it will aid in your discipleship journey.

The daily practice of spending time with God via Bible-reading and prayer, and perhaps a few other spiritual disciplines, is known by many names: quiet time, personal Bible study, personal devotions, morning watch, appointment with God, etc. Whatever you call it, reading the Bible on a regular basis is good for you. Going through this booklet of devotionals is a great start!

Psalm 119, one of many songs and poems in the Bible, celebrates the goodness of God's written word. Virtually all of its 144 verses – yes, it's the longest psalm in the Bible – praise the scriptures. (Note: when the author uses words like "law," "statutes" and "precepts," he's referring to the Old Testament or Torah; most likely its first five books, known as the Pentateuch. Basically, it's the Bible as it existed at the time this psalm was written). It's so lovely, he thinks about it all day; it offers wisdom and insight; it keeps him on the right path.

While it's beneficial to regularly read the Bible, it's even better to understand what it is you're reading. Otherwise, you won't have true insight; you won't really "have more understanding than the elders." The Bible is a collection of books that were written during very different times in very

Growing as a Christian

different cultures; it's possible and important to figure out, but it takes time and resources. Secondary sources such as the excellent preaching we hear at weekend services, commentaries, etc., will accelerate your understanding. The ability to interpret scripture can be developed alongside the more straightforward discipline of simply reading the Bible each day. Incorporate the two and see where it takes you!

For reflection:

Begin devoting 15 minutes per day to Bible-reading. Pick a time that works for you: morning, bedtime, lunch break, your kids' naptime, etc. Many people do this in conjunction with their prayer time. There are many fruitful ways to read the Bible; starting with Genesis and trying to read straight through is not one of them. You'll get bogged down by some of the repetitive, hard-to-understand, and, honestly, rather boring parts of the Old Testament. At the same time, or after you finish this devotional booklet, here are a few approaches to try:

- Follow-up Bible studies: These five-day studies will enhance your understanding of the main themes of the weekend sermon at Vineyard Columbus. Find them on the back of the paper outline or at vineyardcolumbus.org at the "Watch & Listen" page.

- Daily Bible-reading plans: Visit navigators.org/resource/bible-reading-plans/ for several good options.

- Here are some secondary books to consider adding to your Bible-reading routine:
    - 30 Days to Understanding the Bible by Max Anders
    - The ...For Everyone series on the New Testament by N.T. Wright.

Notes & Reflections

Growing as a Christian
2.4 Giving
Matthew 6:19-21

19 "Do not store up for yourselves treasures on earth, where moths and vermin destroy, and where thieves break in and steal. **20** But store up for yourselves treasures in heaven, where moths and vermin do not destroy, and where thieves do not break in and steal. **21** For where your treasure is, there your heart will be also."

Bring to mind the things in your life that have required financial discipline and sacrifice: buying your first car, saving up for an engagement ring, putting yourself through college, a long awaited vacation, fertility treatments, Christmas presents for your kids, a down payment on a house, etc. Chances are, part of the reason you highly appreciate these things is because of what they cost you. To devalue them would be like confessing you threw your money away.

Meanwhile, when something comes to us for free, we tend to have less appreciation for it. Here's another way to look at it: the person who works hard through diet and exercise to maintain a healthy weight, blood sugar level, etc., probably appreciates their wellness much more than the couch potato who doesn't have to do a thing to be thin and healthy.

"For where your treasure is, there your heart will be also." Thousands of years ago, Jesus spoke this truth; something that the above-mentioned personal scenarios echo. Like financially supporting your family, giving to the church is one way to deeply care for your spiritual community. If your money goes toward this community, so will your heart. To love one another and to partner with Christ to heal the world takes financial resources. Each of us give in order to make this happen.

Part of pursuing spiritual maturity involves an awakening of our hearts to generosity and to what really matters in life. We recognize that, like all good things, our money is not our own. It's a gift from God. And what do we do with these blessings, these gifts? We don't hoard them or use them solely for our own gain; we are blessed to be a blessing! What is the best way to be a financial blessing? By investing in things of eternal worth. By partnering with Christ to heal the world, Vineyard Columbus strives to do the work of eternity right here, right now. We minister holistically: whole people – body, mind, and soul, the whole world – social justice, missions, caring for the poor. Our giving is a big part of what makes it all possible.

Now, you may be thinking, "Giving to God? That I have no problem with. Giving to a church is the part I don't like. What if I disagree with how the church uses the money? What if the church turns out to be a corrupt organization?" We hear you. Vineyard Columbus takes many steps to be an excellent steward of the money you give and we strive to be transparent in all of our financial dealings. Every fall, we host a congregational meeting where we open up and discuss our budget and expenditures: salaries and benefits, ministries, property management, debt, etc. Attending these meetings is a great way to learn where the giving goes.

Growing as a Christian

For reflection:

Make a plan to give to God by giving to the church. You can give during the tithes and offerings portion of weekend services, and you can give online at vineyardcolumbus.org or you can text to give at 614-333-0330. You can even sign up to give on a schedule. It will probably take some budgeting, but a great goal is to give 10% of your income on a regular basis; this is called tithing, offering a tenth of all you have.

If giving financially feels out of your league, it's important to understand that God loves you just the same as if you had millions of dollars to give. Giving isn't about currying favor with Jesus; it's about partnering with him to heal the world. And everyone, even lower-income individuals, should get to experience the blessing of doing it. Vineyard Columbus has a wonderful financial ministry that may help make this and other financial freedoms and blessings possible for you on your journey toward spiritual maturity. For more information, email kent.irwin@vineyardcolumbus.org.

Notes & Reflections

Growing as a Christian
Maturity Memory Verses

Philippians 1:6
...being confident of this, that he who began a good work in you will carry it on to completion until the day of Christ Jesus.

Colossians 4:2
Devote yourselves to prayer, being watchful and thankful.

Matthew 4:4
Jesus answered, "It is written: 'Man shall not live on bread alone, but on every word that comes from the mouth of God.'"

Proverbs 3:9
Honor the Lord with your wealth,
    with the firstfruits of all your crops;

Prayer

Lord, I ask you to help me to mature in my relationship with you. Some of the things that make me mature are hard to do or commit to. I need your loving help. Show me how I can grow. Amen

Meeting God

Learning to Walk with Jesus

We Experience God

How can I experience God?

In Revelations 1:4, God is called the "One who was, and is, and who is to come." This section will help you to encounter the God "who is." You'll learn how to experience the Holy Spirit and learn how to follow his lead in praying for healing in people's lives.

Growing as a Christian
3.1 The Holy Spirit
Joel 2:28-29

28 "And afterward,
　I will pour out my Spirit on all people.
Your sons and daughters will prophesy,
　your old men will dream dreams,
　your young men will see visions.
29 Even on my servants, both men and women,
　I will pour out my Spirit in those days.

The Holy Spirit is the one who makes it possible for us to experience God. A person, not a thing, he's part of the trinity with the Father and the Son; he is God. The manifest presence of God, he's the one Jesus promised to us in John 14:26. The Holy Spirit "will teach you all things and will remind you of everything I have said to you." Jesus has ascended to heaven, but the Spirit is here: speaking truth and revelation to us via dreams, prophetic words, etc.; leading us again and again away from the death of sin and toward a life of holiness; empowering us to do miracles as Jesus did. Sometimes, you may even have a physical encounter with him. While praying or worshiping, your hands will get warm and tingly; you may shiver or shake; your throat may get tight. You may even see, hear or smell things of the spiritual realm. It can get a little weird sometimes, but it's a good sort of weird!

Without the Holy Spirit, Christianity becomes more like a club. It lacks the presence and power Jesus promised to us. Don't settle for this. It's not sustainable; we need more. God knows we won't thrive if our relationship with him is a long-distance one. Just consider the challenges of person-to-person long-distance relationships. Via the Holy Spirit, God gets close and personal. In doing so, his holiness and power rub off on us.

In John 14, when Jesus said the Holy Spirit would soon come to his followers, it wasn't the first time God issued such a promise. Hundreds of years earlier, God spoke through the prophet Joel about it: "I will pour out my Spirit on all people." Sons, daughters, men, women, young, old. The Holy Spirit is available to all; experiencing God and his empowerment is not an exclusive club!

Growing as a Christian

When did this outpouring, spoken about by both Joel and Jesus, come to pass? The book of Acts, which chronicles the earliest days of Jesus-followers, tells an amazing story in chapter 2. There, the Holy Spirit comes and something that looked like tongues of fire rested on each person as they began to speak in languages other than their own. On that day, the Apostle Peter declared, "This is what was spoken by the prophet Joel." "Those days" didn't end then; they are still happening now. God wants to pour out his Spirit on you, too!

For reflection:
- Read these verses from Joel out loud and then sit in silence for one minute. Next, invite the Holy Spirit to come and fill you up. Note any sensations you feel or impressions you get. Return to this simple reflection and prayer throughout your day and week. Are there any patterns emerging in the experience? If so, that could be the Holy Spirit. Make seeking to experience God in this way a regular part of your prayer life.

- Sometimes, it's easier to get in touch with the Holy Spirit in a group setting. When believers join together to seek the presence and power of God, he has a tendency to show up. The third Wednesday of each month from 7-9pm, the Cooper Road campus hosts Engage, an evening of worship, intercession, prophecy and prayer ministry time. For more information, email kristi.webster@vineyardcolumbus.org

Meeting God 301
At this class, learn more about experiencing God, the Holy Spirit and the role he plays in your life. See the insert for upcoming dates. For more information, visit https://www.vineyardcolumbus.org/next-steps

Notes & Reflections

Growing as a Christian

3.2 The Already and the Not Yet – Matthew 6:9-13

9 This, then, is how you should pray:
'"Our Father in heaven,
hallowed be your name,
10 your kingdom come,
your will be done,
  on earth as it is in heaven.
11 Give us today our daily bread.
12 And forgive us our debts,
  as we also have forgiven our debtors.
13 And lead us not into temptation,
  but deliver us from the evil one.'

We live in an age of "The Already and the Not Yet." Formally known as "inaugurated eschatology," it's a belief that, thanks to Jesus' life, death and resurrection, we can sometimes glimpse and experience the perfect age to come, the "happily ever after," the resurrection life, the second coming of Christ. When Jesus returns, not only will death, suffering and sorrow be no more, but our relationship with God will be one of pure trust, perfect knowledge and deep, mutual love. We will be face-to-face with Jesus. But what exactly can we expect now, in this present age between Jesus' first and second coming? Do we simply muddle through the hardships of life, looking forward to heaven? Not exactly. The lines between the present age and the age to come sometimes blur. Heaven can come down now!

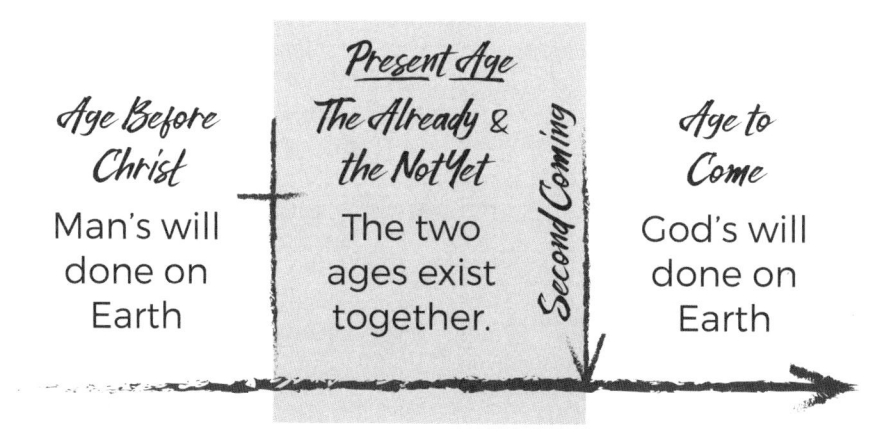

Age Before Christ	Present Age — The Already & the Not Yet	Second Coming	Age to Come
Man's will done on Earth	The two ages exist together.		God's will done on Earth

Powerfully experiencing God is something we can and should expect today; it's one taste of the age to come. Other morsels include miraculous healing, freedom from oppression, reconciliation of relationships, etc. But it's not

Learning to Walk with Jesus

Growing as a Christian

an endless feast on this side of eternity. More often than not, your loved one isn't healed; sometimes, tragedy strikes. These are the "not yet" components of the present age. The breakthrough you desire is going to happen; just "not yet." Desiring the resurrection life right now and for all things is an indicator that God has designed us for eternity. This hunger is what keeps us asking God for more. A great prayer of desire to taste the age to come is, "More, Lord!" As long as we live in this blurred, dotted-line age, never stop asking God for more breakthroughs!

Asking for more of the age to come is exactly what Jesus tells us to do in The Lord's Prayer. "Your kingdom come, your will be done, on earth as it is in heaven" is not a petition for Jesus to come back and take us all to heaven. Rather, it's a prayer for good to conquer evil here on earth, right now. It's a plea for God to invade the earth with his love. God's kingdom come on earth and his will done here would mean no more disease, hunger, war, poverty, abuse, death, etc. The news media would report nothing but good news. We pray this prayer for specific situations, like a loved one's cancer diagnosis. And we pray it for the world, for global poverty to end, etc.

For reflection:

Everyday this week, pray Matthew 6:10. For each day, focus on a different problem in desperate need of God's intervention. It could be personal, familial, global, etc. In light of living in "The Already and the Not Yet," pray with expectancy coupled with appropriate uncertainty. Never give up hope that God can break through in any situation and provide a taste of the age to come.

Notes & Reflections

Growing as a Christian
3.3 Hearing God's Voice
Acts 16:6-10

6 Paul and his companions traveled throughout the region of Phrygia and Galatia, having been kept by the Holy Spirit from preaching the word in the province of Asia. **7** When they came to the border of Mysia, they tried to enter Bithynia, but the Spirit of Jesus would not allow them to. **8** So they passed by Mysia and went down to Troas. **9** During the night Paul had a vision of a man of Macedonia standing and begging him, "Come over to Macedonia and help us." **10** After Paul had seen the vision, we got ready at once to leave for Macedonia, concluding that God had called us to preach the gospel to them.

Hearing God's voice is another important component of experiencing him. When we effectively hear God's voice, he tells us how to pray, what to say, how to act, what to do when we're uncertain, etc.

There are several ways God speaks to us. Sometimes, God will speak in just one way. At other times, especially if the matter at hand is really important, he will use multiple avenues to get his point across. These avenues include: scripture, dreams, visions and distinct thoughts or impressions. Even an unexpected experience or situation may be God's way of getting your attention. Sometimes, a friend will have a dream or vision that they believe is from God and intended for you. While certainly possible, God will rarely, if ever, speak to you in an audible voice. It's usually a little more nuanced than that. If we're too distracted by other things, we may miss the message.

Here in Acts 16, Paul didn't miss God's message. In verse 7, it seems he and his companions, while responding to the call to preach the Gospel to non-Jews, experienced something unexpected. Surely they were wondering what the Holy Spirit was up to when he kept them out of Bithynia. Perhaps that night they fasted and prayed, asking God what it all meant. Then in verses 9-10 the answer comes: Paul has a vision and they decide it meant they needed to bring the Good News of Jesus to Macedonia instead.

Discerning God's voice in bits and pieces like this is not something that happens only in Bible stories. It's an experience you can have today. Many believers today have stories that are just as powerful and pivotal as what Paul experienced in Acts 16. Perhaps your own experience of it

Growing as a Christian

will be the next one added to the collection of God's people hearing his voice!

Here are a few guidelines for discerning the voice of God:
Does it line up with scripture? God would never speak in contradiction of his written word.
Is it something God has spoken to you about before? If you sense a pattern emerging, it may be from God.
What do mature Christians think? A wise friend can provide counsel and confirmation.

After evaluating what you think God is telling you, the only thing left to do is step out in faith and follow his lead. Vineyard movement founder John Wimber is known for saying faith is spelled R-I-S-K. Ask God for his continued wisdom and direction, then take the risk. It may not go as hoped; we can't always hear perfectly from God on this side of eternity; but you won't know until you try!

For reflection:

- You can practice hearing God's voice in spontaneous ways. As you go through your day today or tomorrow, whenever you encounter someone, silently pray, "Lord, is there anything you want me to say or do for this person?" God may speak in an instant, giving you a strong sense of how to respond. To build upon the idea of taking risks, we like to say that risk is spelled T-R-Y. Take the risk and do what you think he's asking of you.

- Bring to mind an important decision or event you have coming up within the next six months. Ask God to speak into the situation. Then, sit in silence for one minute. Repeat this prayer a few times per week. Also ask God to give you dreams and visions regarding the matter, along with words of confirmation from others. Journal any impressions you get and see if a consistent message is emerging.

Notes & Reflections

Growing as a Christian

3.4 Healing & Miracles
Mark 5:21-43

21 When Jesus had again crossed over by boat to the other side of the lake, a large crowd gathered around him while he was by the lake. **22** Then one of the synagogue leaders, named Jairus, came, and when he saw Jesus, he fell at his feet. **23** He pleaded earnestly with him, "My little daughter is dying. Please come and put your hands on her so that she will be healed and live." **24** So Jesus went with him.
A large crowd followed and pressed around him. **25** And a woman was there who had been subject to bleeding for twelve years. **26** She had suffered a great deal under the care of many doctors and had spent all she had, yet instead of getting better she grew worse. **27** When she heard about Jesus, she came up behind him in the crowd and touched his cloak, **28** because she thought, "If I just touch his clothes, I will be healed." **29** Immediately her bleeding stopped and she felt in her body that she was freed from her suffering.
30 At once Jesus realized that power had gone out from him. He turned around in the crowd and asked, "Who touched my clothes?"
31 "You see the people crowding against you," his disciples answered, "and yet you can ask, 'Who touched me?' "
32 But Jesus kept looking around to see who had done it.
33 Then the woman, knowing what had happened to her, came and fell at his feet and, trembling with fear, told him the whole truth. **34** He said to her, "Daughter, your faith has healed you. Go in peace and be freed from your suffering."
35 While Jesus was still speaking, some people came from the house of Jairus, the synagogue leader. "Your daughter is dead," they said. "Why bother the teacher anymore?"
36 Overhearing what they said, Jesus told him, "Don't be afraid; just believe."
37 He did not let anyone follow him except Peter, James and John the brother of James. **38** When they came to the

home of the synagogue leader, Jesus saw a commotion, with people crying and wailing loudly. **39** He went in and said to them, "Why all this commotion and wailing? The child is not dead but asleep." **40** But they laughed at him. After he put them all out, he took the child's father and mother and the disciples who were with him, and went in where the child was. **41** He took her by the hand and said to her, "Talitha koum!" (which means "Little girl, I say to you, get up!").**42** Immediately the girl stood up and began to walk around (she was twelve years old). At this they were completely astonished. **43** He gave strict orders not to let anyone know about this, and told them to give her something to eat.

Do you believe in divine healing? The kind of healing that comes via prayer and God's direct intervention? Permanent hearing loss is restored. The tumor has disappeared. Or what about miracles? Someone's bank account is in the negative, and rent is due tomorrow. An envelope of cash, containing the exact amount needed to pay the landlord, appears in the mailbox the next morning.

Christians ought to believe in divine healing and miracles. Moreover, we should partner with God to do the work of healing and miracles. From Moses to the prophet Elijah to Jesus to his followers, the Bible has an abundance of miracle stories. As for divine healing, it was one of the primary components of Jesus' public ministry. These occurrences in the Bible aren't just thrilling stories to read; they are things that can happen today, with God using us as a vessel for his power.

In this story from Mark, we get a two-for-one deal. While Jesus is en route to heal one person, he kinda sorta accidentally heals another. Pretty cool! This story illustrates several things:
1.   Desperation is good. Jairus falls at Jesus' feet and pleads

Growing as a Christian

with him. Approaching God like this isn't pathetic, it's beautiful!
2. Divine healings and miracles don't always happen in the way we expect. Don't let an interruption or the unexpected stop you from experiencing God via healing and miracles, both for yourself and others.
3. Jesus' healing is often multi-faceted. The woman subject to long-term bleeding was not only physically healed, but she also experienced financial, mental, societal and relational restoration. Doctor bills, being ceremonially unclean, the fear of making others unclean, etc. were now a thing of her past. God is a holistic healer. He loves us that much!
4. God is always on time and always has enough resources. Waylaid by the hemorrhaging woman, it seems Jesus is too late to help the sick little girl. "Why bother?" the people say. But bother he does, and he raises the girl to life. It's never too late for a miracle or divine healing. And it never bothers God when we ask.

We shouldn't keep experiences of divine healing and miracles to ourselves. They're not just for Christians, they're for the whole world. All of creation gets to experience God in these ways when we are obedient to his call to heal the sick and perform miracles. Via the scriptures, Jesus is essentially saying to each of us, "I've shown you how to do it. Now, you do it."

For reflection:

- This particular aspect of experiencing God – divine healing and miracles – is a lot to take in. It's a little "out there," isn't it? Take a moment now to consider your reaction to the possibility that God can move in these ways, especially through you. Share your thoughts with God.
- One of the best ways to begin seeking God for healing and miracles is to ask someone with experience to pray for you about a physical affliction, need for a miracle,

etc. This person will lay their hands on you and pray "in the name of Jesus" for you to be well or for the miracle to occur. Also ask the person if you can pray together for someone else in need of healing. Praying alongside someone with more experience is a great way to learn how to do the work of healing and miracles!

Notes & Reflections

Growing as a Christian
Meeting God Memory Verses

John 15:26
When the Advocate comes, whom I will send to you from the Father—the Spirit of truth who goes out from the Father—he will testify about me.

Luke 17:20-21
20 Once, on being asked by the Pharisees when the kingdom of God would come, Jesus replied, "The coming of the kingdom of God is not something that can be observed, **21** nor will people say, 'Here it is,' or 'There it is,' because the kingdom of God is in your midst."

John 10:27
My sheep listen to my voice; I know them, and they follow me.

John 14:12
Very truly I tell you, whoever believes in me will do the works I have been doing, and they will do even greater things than these, because I am going to the Father.

Prayer

Lord, I pray to experience you more in my life. I ask that you would show me how limitless you are in this world, my life, and the lives of those I pray for. And where it is hard for me to believe, I ask for you to help my disbelief. Amen

Ministry

Learning to Walk with Jesus

We Love One Another

How do I love the church and others?

As followers of Jesus, we are all called to serve and help one another according to the unique way God has designed each and every one of us. These devotionals will help you learn more about your gifts and what God has in store for you.

Growing as a Christian

4.1 Calling
Mark 1:16-20

16 As Jesus walked beside the Sea of Galilee, he saw Simon and his brother Andrew casting a net into the lake, for they were fishermen. **17** "Come, follow me," Jesus said, "and I will send you out to fish for people." **18** At once they left their nets and followed him.

19 When he had gone a little farther, he saw James son of Zebedee and his brother John in a boat, preparing their nets. **20** Without delay he called them, and they left their father Zebedee in the boat with the hired men and followed him.

Learning to Walk with Jesus

Some kids have big dreams for what they want to be when they grow up. Movie star, professional athlete, famous musician, etc. Some modern twists likely include celebrity chef, professional gamer, computer animator, YouTube star, etc. Do kids feel like these are their callings in life? Maybe, but more likely, these dreams are probably just that: exciting daydreams that are fun to act out and draw pictures of.

As adults, many of us feel called to things that are important, but not quite as shiny as our childhood dreams: parenthood, a career that makes a difference, run a 5k, declutter the entire house, etc. When it comes to following Jesus, calling works a little bit differently. Before we are called to something, we are called to someone.

When Jesus called his first disciples, they were in the middle of doing something else: fishing. In this moment, Jesus completely changed the course of their lives. The disciples could've passed Jesus up on his offer or said, "Ask me again in six months." But instead, they follow him "at once." This isn't because they were prone to impulsivity. Rather, it's because once you encounter his presence and begin to understand who he really is, it's hard to resist Jesus.

It's important to understand that no ministry, no act of love for others, no service will go the way you desire if you don't first say yes when Jesus calls you to himself. The first call you said yes to is when you initially give your life to Christ. The echo of this call comes again and again, everyday, in every moment. When things aren't going well at work, Jesus says, "Come, follow me." When parenting consumes your every waking (and non-waking!) moment, Jesus says, "Come,

Growing as a Christian

follow me." When your to-do list is a mile long, Jesus says, "Come, follow me."

For reflection:

- In what ways do you sense Jesus calling you to himself? Imagine Jesus approaching you and saying, "Come, follow me." Try to vividly picture the scene. What are you doing when he approaches you? What is his body language and tone of voice like? Yours? What comes to mind as you consider his offer? Now, imagine your response. What do you say? What do you do? Throughout your days, especially when you feel overwhelmed or unsure of what to prioritize or how to proceed, picture Jesus calling you to himself. Let this reflection be a pathway to peace and focus.

Ministry 401

As followers of Jesus, we are all called to serve. In this class, you'll learn more about your unique gifts and what God has in store for you. See the insert for upcoming dates. For more information, visit https://www.vineyardcolumbus.org/next-steps

Notes & Reflections

Growing as a Christian

4.2 Gifting
Romans 12:3-8

3 For by the grace given me I say to every one of you: Do not think of yourself more highly than you ought, but rather think of yourself with sober judgment, in accordance with the faith God has distributed to each of you. **4** For just as each of us has one body with many members, and these members do not all have the same function, **5** so in Christ we, though many, form one body, and each member belongs to all the others. **6** We have different gifts, according to the grace given to each of us. If your gift is prophesying, then prophesy in accordance with your faith; **7** if it is serving, then serve; if it is teaching, then teach; **8** if it is to encourage, then give encouragement; if it is giving, then give generously; if it is to lead, do it diligently; if it is to show mercy, do it cheerfully.

In the song Feels Like Christmas, Straight No Chaser sings, "When I'm with you it feels like Christmas, I must have been good, cuz baby you're just what I wanted." These words convey a common misunderstanding of what a gift is. If you think that in exchange for your self-perceived goodness you deserve something like romance, that's a trade. It's not a gift. Perhaps this group should heed Paul's words here in Romans 12:3: "Do not think of yourself more highly than you ought, but rather think of yourself with sober judgment." A more accurate lyric, one with sober judgment, would go something like this: "God must be so good to have given me such an amazing gift."

By definition, the noun "gift" means two different things: "a notable capacity, talent or endowment" and "something voluntarily transferred from one person to another without compensation." When it comes to the gifts God gives to us, both definitions fit the bill! He pours out on us a notable spiritual capacity to do amazing things, to fulfill our unique calling. It's his love and his grace alone that cause them to materialize in our lives. Spiritual gifts aren't of our own creation or effort. Paul conveys this truth a few chapters prior in Romans 9:16: "It does not, therefore, depend on human desire or effort, but on God's mercy."

Let's examine Paul's discussion of spiritual gifts here in Romans 12. Verses 3-6 instruct us on how to approach spiritual gifts: with humility and selflessness, and an eye toward how they can benefit others. We are blessed with spiritual gifts in order to be a blessing to others. In verses 6-8, Paul lists some specific spiritual gifts: prophecy, service, teaching, encouragement, generosity, leadership and mercy. This is not an exhaustive list. Other mentions of

Growing as a Christian

different spiritual gifts in scripture include 1 Corinthians 12:7-11, 27-31 and 1 Peter 4:10-11.

Maybe you are wondering about your own spiritual gifts. Do you have any, even one? What are they? The good news is God has given everyone spiritual gifts. He hasn't skipped over you or anyone else. He is a good, impartial father who loves giving gifts to all of his children. What's more, there are some great methods and resources for identifying your spiritual gifts. It's also important to remember that spiritual gifts are not static. Some gifts you may possess your entire life, such as teaching. As for others, God may temporarily dispense a gift such as healing or prophecy for a specific moment. It's an adventurous joy to receive, exercise, and give away spiritual gifts!

For reflection:

- Using Romans 12, 1 Corinthians 12 and 1 Peter 4 as a guide, begin to regularly pray for spiritual gifts. Paul tells us to "eagerly desire the greater gifts." God loves giving gifts to his children; he wants us to ask for them.

- Complete the spiritual gifts assessment at the Ministry 401 class. As you learn to identify and demonstrate the spiritual gifts God's given you, pray for grace to faithfully give them away.

Notes & Reflections

Growing as a Christian
4.3 Service
John 13:1-17

1 It was just before the Passover Festival. Jesus knew that the hour had come for him to leave this world and go to the Father. Having loved his own who were in the world, he loved them to the end.
2 The evening meal was in progress, and the devil had already prompted Judas, the son of Simon Iscariot, to betray Jesus. **3** Jesus knew that the Father had put all things under his power, and that he had come from God and was returning to God;**4** so he got up from the meal, took off his outer clothing, and wrapped a towel around his waist. **5** After that, he poured water into a basin and began to wash his disciples' feet, drying them with the towel that was wrapped around him.
6 He came to Simon Peter, who said to him, "Lord, are you going to wash my feet?"
7 Jesus replied, "You do not realize now what I am doing, but later you will understand."
8 "No," said Peter, "you shall never wash my feet."
Jesus answered, "Unless I wash you, you have no part with me."
9 "Then, Lord," Simon Peter replied, "not just my feet but my hands and my head as well!"
10 Jesus answered, "Those who have had a bath need only to wash their feet; their whole body is clean. And you are clean, though not every one of you." **11** For he knew who was going to betray him, and that was why he said not every one was clean.
12 When he had finished washing their feet, he put on his clothes and returned to his place. "Do you understand what I have done for you?" he asked them. **13** "You call me 'Teacher' and 'Lord,' and rightly so, for that is what I am. **14** Now that I, your Lord and Teacher, have washed your feet, you also should wash one another's feet. **15** I have set you an

example that you should do as I have done for you. **16** Very truly I tell you, no servant is greater than his master, nor is a messenger greater than the one who sent him. **17** Now that you know these things, you will be blessed if you do them.

As we begin exploring our unique passions and spiritual gifts, and learn how to express them in this world, we should take a step back to consider what the point is. It's not to garner power or prestige. Nor are these things done out of a sense of obligation. Rather, it's love. This isn't the "feeling in your heart" variety of love. It's an active expression of love. This is what service is all about. Fulfilling your calling and exercising your spiritual gifts should culminate in loving people the way Jesus did.

Jesus is the very best model of love in action. If he were alive today, his demonstration of love for others wouldn't begin and end with retweeting compelling quotes about social justice. He wouldn't serve others only when it was easy and convenient for him. The way Jesus loves people by serving them is astounding. He loves "to the end" (verse 1). He serves in a way so extravagant and loving that it can seem inappropriate. Sometimes, we don't even know how to respond! This is Peter in verses 6-9 of this story. He is all over the place with his emotions and his understanding of what Jesus is communicating by washing his disciples' feet. This is an incredible moment of foreshadowing: by kneeling down to do something humiliating and far beneath him – footwashing – and then "returning to his place" (verse 12), Jesus is pointing to his death and resurrection.

Let's reflect on verses 14-17. We are to follow Jesus' example and serve others, even, or perhaps especially, if it requires us to get low, to assume a position that's much humbler than we're used to. Jesus-style service is also very personal and relational. There's a big difference between kneeling down to wash someone's feet and donating to a charity. By no

Growing as a Christian

means is the latter trivial or something to avoid; it's just not the highly relational example Jesus gives to us here in John 13. Between these two factors – to suppress our pride and truly serve others, and doing it while encountering people very personally – it may feel awkward and messy. That's OK; Jesus is in the awkwardness and mess.

Service doesn't benefit only the recipient. It's great for the giver, too. When we serve, we are reminded of the calling God has on our life, we get a chance to use our spiritual gifts, and, in a very tangible way, we are put back in touch with how much Jesus loves us and has served us.

For reflection:

- Instead of saying to Jesus, "You shall never serve me!", a paraphrase of what Peter said to him in verse 8, allow Jesus to love you and serve you. In what areas of your life do you keep Jesus on the top shelf, out of reach of the messiness of your life? Let him sink his hands into the muddy mess and help you out. It could be about your relationships, finances, a sin struggle, etc. Call on God to take care of you as only he can.

- Bolstered by a deep awareness of how much God loves you and delights in serving you, go out and serve people as Jesus would. A great place to start is via a ministry at church. There are many opportunities to serve that will line up with your interests and spiritual gifts. So many of our ministries are at their core focused on serving others as we believe Jesus would: Community Outreach, Transitions, Value Life, VineyardKids, etc. To explore volunteer opportunities for all the different ministries, visit https://www.vineyardcolumbus.org/ministries/
For more information, email diane.bauman@vineyardcolumbus.org.

Notes & Reflections

Growing as a Christian
4.4 Wherever You Are
Matthew 5:13-16

13 "You are the salt of the earth. But if the salt loses its saltiness, how can it be made salty again? It is no longer good for anything, except to be thrown out and trampled underfoot.
14 "You are the light of the world. A town built on a hill cannot be hidden. **15** Neither do people light a lamp and put it under a bowl. Instead they put it on its stand, and it gives light to everyone in the house. **16** In the same way, let your light shine before others, that they may see your good deeds and glorify your Father in heaven.

Once you have a sense of your calling and become familiar with your spiritual gifts, you'll understand that serving others should be one of your highest goals. This is the journey you're on in discovering your God-given ministry. But exactly where and when does this journey happen? It's not just within church walls; nor is it among only your Christian friends. Jesus wants us to understand that ministering to others happens wherever you happen to be.

What does it look like? What is the vibe of walking out your ministry – calling, gifting, and service – when you're at work, at the grocery store, putting your kids to bed, chatting with your neighbor, etc.? First, the vibe is salty. In this context, we're definitely not talking about the slang definition of salty: to be upset. Rather, it means you are to add good flavor to the world and to bring out the best of whomever and whatever is around you. When you are faithful to God's calling, when you give away your spiritual gifts, and when you regularly serve others, you are the salt of the earth. A word of encouragement helps bring out someone's best. Giving away a gift such as healing definitely helps someone to be their best. Go ahead, add good flavor to the world!

And what does it mean to be the light of the world regarding your ministry? By letting your light shine, you aren't hiding the source of your passion, what drives you. When people realize that Jesus is the reason you do what you do, they won't just think you're an exceptional person; they will realize God is the reason and "glorify him in heaven." Sometimes Christians get into a habit of hiding or covering their light. A person may shine the light of Jesus at church and in the workplace, but rarely with family. And forget about letting your light shine in situations where it

Growing as a Christian

may be awkward. We should resist the temptation to cover our light. Like something that's completely transparent, Jesus' light should shine through us in all situations

Strive to actually be what Jesus says you are: salt of the earth and light of the world. Wherever you are, be these things. In every moment, look for ways to express your calling, give away your gifts and serve others.

For reflection:

- This week, select one slice of your life to practice intentionally being salt and light. Consider your workplace, your college campus, your neighborhood, etc. What is one way you can bring out the best in a person or a situation in this setting? How can you shine the light of God's goodness? Pray that God would go ahead of you and give you the determination to be salt and light wherever you are.

Notes & Reflections

Growing as a Christian
Ministry Memory Verses

Romans 8:28
And we know that in all things God works for the good of those who love him, who have been called according to his purpose.

1 Peter 4:10
Each of you should use whatever gift you have received to serve others, as faithful stewards of God's grace in its various forms.

John 15:12-13
12 My command is this: Love each other as I have loved you. **13** Greater love has no one than this: to lay down one's life for one's friends.

1 Corinthians 15:58
Therefore, my dear brothers and sisters, stand firm. Let nothing move you. Always give yourselves fully to the work of the Lord, because you know that your labor in the Lord is not in vain.

Prayer

God, thank you for how you created me, for all of the gifts you have given to me. I ask Lord, that you help me discover how I can use these gifts to serve you, my community and the world. Amen

Mission

Learning to Walk with Jesus

We Partner with Christ to Heal the World

How do I love the world?

Jesus is the total package. He came sharing Good News with the poor, forgiving, healing the sick and providing freedom to the burdened and battered. These devotionals will paint a picture of what role you can play.

Growing as a Christian
5.1 Holistic Mission 101
Luke 4:14-21

14 Jesus returned to Galilee in the power of the Spirit, and news about him spread through the whole countryside. **15** He was teaching in their synagogues, and everyone praised him.

16 He went to Nazareth, where he had been brought up, and on the Sabbath day he went into the synagogue, as was his custom. He stood up to read, **17** and the scroll of the prophet Isaiah was handed to him. Unrolling it, he found the place where it is written:

18 "The Spirit of the Lord is on me,
 because he has anointed me
 to proclaim good news to the poor.
He has sent me to proclaim freedom for the prisoners
 and recovery of sight for the blind,
to set the oppressed free,
19 to proclaim the year of the Lord's favor."

20 Then he rolled up the scroll, gave it back to the attendant and sat down. The eyes of everyone in the synagogue were fastened on him. **21** He began by saying to them, "Today this scripture is fulfilled in your hearing."

This is Jesus' mic drop moment. He's telling everyone why he came; he's explaining his mission. God certainly wants us to spend eternity in relationship with him, but he also cares about everything he's created. And he wants every part of us – body, mind, and spirit – to be healed and whole. He desires for us to have thriving relationships and dignified, meaningful work. He intends for there to be peace and harmony at every level of creation, from the interpersonal to the global. He wants the planet and all life on it to abound in wellness.

Clearly, Jesus' mission is not narrow; it's a holistic one to "proclaim the year of the Lord's favor." This is a nod to the year of Jubilee, a very special time that came just once every 49 years for the Jewish people. In that year, prisoners and slaves would be freed and debts would be forgiven. God's mercies and goodness would often fall heavily on his people. Jesus' mission is to inaugurate the full, eternal completion of Jubilee. In his coming to earth, the year of Jubilee, "the year of the Lord's favor," is here for good!

What exactly does this mean? It means proclaiming and demonstrating to the poor that the spiritual riches of God are theirs for the taking. It means working to eradicate poverty and its harmful impact on individuals, families and societies. It means seeking the freedom of those imprisoned by addiction, disease, demonic strongholds, etc. It means opening the eyes of the spiritually blind to God's love. It means healing the physically blind. It means seeking liberation for those oppressed by sexism, racism, social injustice, etc. Jesus' holistic mission is awesome! It's for everyone and everything!

Growing as a Christian

For reflection:

- Imagine the scene in Luke 4:20: "The eyes of everyone in the synagogue were fastened on him." It's a quite fitting response to this mic-dropping mission-announcing moment in Jesus' ministry. But the truth is we should always keep our eyes fastened on Jesus. If we want to be more like him and partner with him to heal the world, he needs to be our central focus. If you haven't started regularly praying and reading the Bible, now is a great time to start! As you pray, spend time simply picturing Jesus before you. As you read the Bible, pay special attention to all the ways he ushers in the year of the Lord's favor.

- Write down some ways you can partner with Christ to proclaim the year of the Lord's favor and be a Jubilee-presence in this weary world. The prior section on Ministry may have given you some ideas already. What hurts and injustices in the world particularly stir up compassion within your heart? What resources and gifts do you bring to the table to help alleviate them? Pray God would begin to make your mission path clear and that you'd be faithful to take the first step.

Mission 501

Jesus came sharing Good News with the poor, forgiving, healing the sick and providing freedom to the burdened and battered. In this class, learn how to share the healing message of Jesus by your words and deeds. See the insert for upcoming dates. For more information, visit https://www.vineyardcolumbus.org/next-steps

Notes & Reflections

Growing as a Christian

5.2 Evangelism & World Missions
Matthew 28:18-20

18 Then Jesus came to them and said, "All authority in heaven and on earth has been given to me. **19** Therefore go and make disciples of all nations, baptizing them in the name of the Father and of the Son and of the Holy Spirit, **20** and teaching them to obey everything I have commanded you. And surely I am with you always, to the very end of the age."

God's love for each and every person he's ever created is tremendous. When you dearly love someone, what is your hope? It's to spend as much time as possible with the person and to see them thrive. This is why, here at the end of the gospel of Matthew, Jesus calls us to draw people to himself. These are some of his very last words to his followers. Last words tend to be important.

Moreover, the more followers of Jesus there are in the world, the more hearts, hands and feet there are to do God's missional work. God not only loves everyone but he has a unique plan for the role each person will play in fulfilling his mission. Multiplying the number of people who follow Jesus add to the number of those who deeply experience God's love and partner with him to heal the world. The more, the merrier!

Evangelism is quite misunderstood, even vilified these days. Opportunities to restore it to its original purpose, the one Jesus explained to us, are abundant. To evangelize means to be the bearer of Good News in both word and deed. Never should it be about indoctrinating someone with a political ideology or "American values." That's not healing. Nor should it be about simply converting someone. Jesus told us to "make disciples," not "converts." You are on your own discipleship journey; when you evangelize someone you invite them into all of its milestones: saying yes to Jesus; becoming part of a church community; maturing in Christ and learning to be like him; experiencing him; loving others and healing the world. Discipleship is so much more than a single moment of conversion!

World missions are a natural expression of evangelism. Jesus

Growing as a Christian

tells us to "make disciples of all nations." We aren't called to make disciples only of people who look like us, live near us, speak like us, act like us, etc. There are no boundary lines on God's love for people. Moreover, if Christians don't engage in world missions, there are some people groups who may never learn about Jesus and his mission to heal the entire world. Christians are called to be Good News-bearers across the globe.

Making disciples isn't about finding people to follow us, to join our church, and to think and act like we do. We make disciples because we want everyone to know Jesus. As followers of Jesus, and disciples ourselves, we are called to love everyone. When you love someone, you want the best for them. And since Jesus is the best and has the best to offer the world, we evangelize; we make disciples.

For reflection:

- Jesus frames his command to make disciples with some great assurances: "All authority in heaven and on earth has been given to me" and "surely I am with you always, to the very end of the age." Jesus, who has power over everything and can do anything, is with us! When you share the Good News with a loved one, Jesus is with you. When you pray for a sick friend who doesn't follow Jesus, Jesus is with you. This week, believing in Jesus' assurances, write down one thing you can do to be a Good News-bearer. He will empower you; he will always be with you.
-
- God may not call you to become a missionary, but we all have a role to play in supporting world missions. Visit https://www.vineyardcolumbus.org/ministries/international-ministries/ to learn more about the different roles that need filled. You can pray for missionaries, financially support them, volunteer to serve immigrants in your own community, etc.

Notes & Reflections

Growing as a Christian

5.3 Justice & Mercy Micah 6:6-8

6 With what shall I come before the Lord
   and bow down before the exalted God?
Shall I come before him with burnt offerings,
   with calves a year old?
7 Will the Lord be pleased with thousands of rams,
   with ten thousand rivers of olive oil?
Shall I offer my firstborn for my transgression,
   the fruit of my body for the sin of my soul?
8 He has shown you, O mortal, what is good.
   And what does the Lord require of you?
To act justly and to love mercy
   and to walk humbly with your God.

Sometimes, when you know the truth about something, you forget about virtues like kindness and humility. The urge to prove you are right can override decency and civility. Kids often do this, but so do adults. Just look at the comments section of many online articles!

Today's passage is from the Old Testament prophet Micah. He spoke on God's behalf to the people hundreds of years prior to Jesus' arrival, during a time when ritual sacrifice was one of the key ways to worship God. You could offer sacrifices of thanksgiving or devotion, to atone for your sin, etc. People usually sacrificed their animals or their crops, which the priests then ate. While animal sacrifice or donating barrels of olive oil aren't things very relevant to us today, the message in verse 8 is timeless.

When we partner with Christ to heal the world, we ought to do so in humility with hearts, words, and actions abounding in grace and mercy. These are the characteristics that God wants all of his followers across the world, across all of time to exude. These are the offerings that please him. God doesn't want people to be arrogant, harsh, and more focused on being right rather than loving when they partner with him in mission. Proving you are right, trying to pound the truth of the Good News into people, and attacking those who don't agree are all methods God rejects. If we're not willing to do what he calls good when we partner with him in mission – act justly, love mercy, and walk humbly – we might as well not do it at all.

This is another aspect of the "Both-And" nature of God. Yes, through evangelism and missions Christians share good, truthful news with people, but we must do it with

Growing as a Christian

humility, and in a way that cares about the whole person and about all of creation. This is what God requires of us. To "act justly" means to restore social justice so that the poor and disenfranchised are treated with love and respect, as God intends. To "love mercy" means to show compassion or forgiveness toward someone, even when you are in the right. "To walk humbly with your God" means to take a low position, to think of yourself less and to think of God more. Justice, mercy and humility are essential components of God's mission.

For reflection:

- In 1 Corinthians 13, the Apostle Paul says, if he does "not have love, I am only a resounding gong or a clanging cymbal." In moments when you may sound like only harsh noise, pause and consider whether love is motivating you. Tempted to leave a snarky comment on someone's Facebook post? Tempted to be a discourteous driver toward someone with a political bumper sticker that irks you? Pray God would speak to you in those moments, asking you, "Are you acting in love, justice, mercy and humility?" In all your interactions, especially as you intentionally try to demonstrate Jesus to people in word and deed, allow God to probe you with this question.

Notes & Reflections

Growing as a Christian

5.4 Holistic Mission 201
Jeremiah 29:4-7

4 This is what the Lord Almighty, the God of Israel, says to all those I carried into exile from Jerusalem to Babylon: **5** "Build houses and settle down; plant gardens and eat what they produce. **6** Marry and have sons and daughters; find wives for your sons and give your daughters in marriage, so that they too may have sons and daughters. Increase in number there; do not decrease. **7** Also, seek the peace and prosperity of the city to which I have carried you into exile. Pray to the Lord for it, because if it prospers, you too will prosper."

"Think globally, act locally" is a phrase used in various contexts. Everyone from businesspeople to activists have used it. Essentially, it urges people to consider the health of the whole for every decision and action they take. For a business, this would mean considering the vitality of the overall corporation when you scrutinize line items in the budget or hire a new department director. For the environmental activist, this means banning plastic bags in your house and biking instead of driving so you don't contribute to pollution across the globe.

What does "think globally, act locally" mean for the Christian who wants to partner with Christ to heal the world? When you exit the parking lot at Vineyard Columbus' Cooper Road campus, you'll see a sign that has this passage from Jeremiah. Of all the Bible verses that could be on a sign in a church parking lot, it seems a little random to feature the words of an Old Testament prophet, right? But if you consider the words more closely, this is one way to "think globally, act locally." When we settle down in our community and seek to be our city's best friend, which is the mission of the Vineyard Community Center, we have the whole of creation in mind and God's mission to heal it, but we act locally. When we actively seek and pray for the prosperity of our communities, we have the peace and prosperity of the whole world in mind.

Sometimes, Christians fall into thinking they must take a vow of poverty, move to a remote area of the majority world, or do some other radical-looking thing in order to partner with Christ to heal the world. But the truth is, for most of us, the mission is a lot simpler on the surface. Be a good neighbor. Volunteer at your child's school. Help someone

Growing as a Christian

load their groceries into their car. As you go about your day, in both planned and spontaneous ways, contribute to the peace and prosperity of your community. Your role in the mission is still holistic – it's still a matter of partnering with Christ to heal the world – but it's locally executed.

For reflection:

- Consider volunteering at the Vineyard Community Center. You can offer a program, teach a class, etc. Even by simply enrolling in classes there and getting to know other people in the community, you are seeking "the peace and prosperity of the city." For more information, visit vineyardcommunitycenter.org.

- Write down some opportunities where you can "think globally, act locally" when it comes to partnering with Christ to heal the world. Consider your neighborhood: make a conscious effort to learn your neighbor's names and find practical ways to seek the peace and prosperity of your block. Help an elderly neighbor take care of her yard and pets. Make your home a hangout spot for the kids and teens in the neighborhood. How can you be your neighborhood's best friend? Consider these opportunities for other areas of your life: your workplace, your child's school, your extended family, etc.

Notes & Reflections

Growing as a Christian
Mission Memory Verses

Isaiah 43:19
See, I am doing a new thing!
　Now it springs up; do you not perceive it?
I am making a way in the wilderness
　and streams in the wasteland.

Acts 1:8
But you will receive power when the Holy Spirit comes on you; and you will be my witnesses in Jerusalem, and in all Judea and Samaria, and to the ends of the earth."

Isaiah 1:17
Learn to do right; seek justice.
　Defend the oppressed.
Take up the cause of the fatherless;
　plead the case of the widow.

1 Corinthians 10:24
No one should seek their own good, but the good of others.

Prayer

God, over the past several weeks, I have been learning how I can walk with you. Thank you for coming into my life. When I had nothing in turn to offer, you still gifted me with salvation, love, talents, and guidance; thank you. Lord, help me to take all of this information and learn how to apply it to my life. Thank you for your grace and mercy for when I don't get it quite right and I mess up. Lord give me a burning desire to love this world, and the wisdom to see how you want me to do it. Amen

Growing as a Christian
Notes & Reflections

Growing as a Christian
Notes & Reflections